The Holy Regeneration

© 2003 by Debora Lee Meehan

Published by:
New Century Press
1055 Bay Boulevard, Suite C
Chula Vista, CA 91911
(800) 519-2465
www.newcenturypress.com
E-mail: sales@newcenturypress.com

Library of Congress Card Number:
2003110960 X-UIDL: 628

ISBN 1-890035-33-5

COVER DESIGN BY NEW CENTURY PRESS

All rights reserved. No part of this book
may be reproduced in any form or by any means
without permission in writing from the author.

10 9 8 7 6 5 4 3 2 1

Mission Statement

My mission is to teach others that it's our God-given right, privilege and responsibility to exercise the principle of stewardship of the temple, which is your mind, body, and soul life. God has devised at conception, by innate ability, for you to understand how to appropriately use the resources in nature to restore health to your mind, body, and soul. Whenever trauma has befallen mind, body or soul, you have been given access to total restoration in order that you may enjoy a full, rich, and abundant life.

Benediction

The most important truth in this life is that God loves us no matter what we do or don't do. His acceptance and love for us is unconditional. My prayer is that you just accept that, please.

In addition to that acceptance, God, the Father of our Lord, Jesus Christ, the Father of glory may give unto you the spirit of wisdom and revelation in the knowledge of Him. The eyes of your understanding being enlightened that ye may know what is the hope of His calling, and what the riches of the glory of His inheritance in the saints, and what the exceeding greatness of His power is toward us who believe according to the working of His mighty power. He wrought in Christ when He raised Him from the dead and set Him at his own right hand in the heavenly places. May the book of Ephesians come into full reality in your life. May we learn and practice the principle of stewardship on this plane for the profit of our spiritual advancement and the evolution of the individual soul.

Dedication

This book is dedicated to the human beings that have the courage to search out the truth concerning colon hygiene. "And all unclean and evil smelling things shall flow out of you as the uncleanness of garments washed in water flow away and are lost in the stream of the river"

To the brave who will wash the cellular memory of the accumulation of the sin and trespasses off the DNA and reprogram it with health and wellness with a higher vibration and frequency.

To the pioneers of the future who seek the energetic abilities that come when the physical body is purified at every level.

To the human being that will not be fearful to leave the old body to die to new life.

To my friend, Angela, one of the bravest people I have ever met, who will complete the full process of colon hygiene, until the water runs clear.

References

TOOTH TRUTH, Frank J. Jerome, D.D.S.

LOVE WITHOUT END, JESUS SPEAKS, Glenda Green

SOUL PSYCHOLOGY, Joshua David Stone, Ph.D.

THE LIGHT SHALL SET YOU FREE, Dr. Norma Milanovich, Dr. Shirley McCune

THE PRAYER OF JABEZ, Bruce Wilkinson

IT'S ALL IN YOUR HEAD, Hal Huggins, D.D.S.

THE CURE FOR ALL DISEASES, Dr. Hulda Clark, Ph.D., N.D.

HEALING THE SHAME THAT BINDS YOU, John Bradshaw

THE FAMILY, John Bradshaw

BACH FLOWER THERAPY, Mechtchild Scheffer

EAT RIGHT FOR YOUR TYPE, Dr. Peter J. D'Adamo with Catherine Whitney

ANATOMY OF THE SPIRIT, Caroline Myss, Ph.D.

DIET FOR A NEW AMERICA, John Robbins

TISSUE CLEANSING THROUGH BOWEL MANAGEMENT, Dr. Bernard Jensen

THE PENDULUM, THE BIBLE, AND YOUR SURVIVAL, Hanna Kroeger

Contents

Truth from Scriptures 3
Free Will 7
The Soul 9
Poverty Consciousness 11
Hypothyroidism 13
The Full Circle of Healing 17
The Great Discrepancy 19
Light Manifests Things in the Darkness 23
Yeast 25
Skin Cancer 27
The Victim Mentality 29
Curing the Common Cold 31
Reprint of V.E. Irons 33
An Arm and a Leg 43
The One and Only Colonic 45
The Unique Tool That Measures 47
The Reed 51
The Big Awakening 53
It's the Real Booty Call 57
The News of the Weird 59
January 2001 61
The Philosophy of One Century is the Common Sense of the Next 65
The Jabez Prayer 69
A Heavy Metals News Flash 71
Process of Discovering Real Personal Wellness 77
Advance Colon Hygiene May Lead To Regeneration 85

Foreword

Truth from Scriptures

My search took me to the book of I Corinthians: 12. I was familiar with these passages of Scripture because during the years spent in the ministry, we studied repeatedly the gift of the Holy Spirit and the gift ministries. God tells us once we have received the Holy Spirit that we can utilize the diversities of operations of the gift. And as verse 7 states, *"But the manifestation of the Spirit it is given to every man to profit withal."* The creator for our utilization has provided the proper tools so that we can come to enjoy abundant life, which would be the ultimate profit to us.

The operations of the gifts are listed in verses 8, 9, 10, and 11. Although all operations are equally important and available, I will focus on two, gifts of healings and working of miracles. As we follow chapter 12 verses 27 through 31, God has set some in the church to be workers of miracles and gifts of healing. So why not take advantage of this reality and truth and become empowered as God intended for us? By taking control of our own health care, we secure the responsibility and accountability of it and are responsible for the outcome of our health, good or bad. We make ultimate decisions for ourselves. God has provided specific information for the carrying out of this responsibility.

In my search for truth, I found this information:

Another witness of early recommendations of colon hydrotherapy is the so-called Essene gospel of peace whose text dates from the 3rd century after Christ. The complete Aramaic manuscript exists in the secret archives of the Vatican, and a translation into old Slavonic is kept in the royal archives of the Hapsburgs, now the property of the republic of Austria.

We owe the existence of these two versions to the historian priests of the Essenes brotherhood who, under pressure of the advancing hoards of Genghis Khan, were forced to flee to the west, bearing all their ancient scriptures and icons.

It is to the merit of the International Biogenic Society of Matskee British Columbia, Canada, founded in 1928 by the philosopher Roman Rolan, Nobel Laureate of 1915, and Edmund Waldo Schecklee, a Hungarian bishop of the Unitarian church. Theologists have compared, edited and translated into English the old manuscripts.

During the more than 70 years since the publication of the translation of the ancient manuscripts, also known as the dead sea scrolls, more than 10 million readers have absorbed the message. Following is a condensed citation of the Essene gospel of peace:

Renew yourselves and fast for I tell you truly that Satan and his plagues may only be cast out by fasting and by prayer. Go by yourself and fast alone and show your fasting to no man. The living God shall see it and great shall be your reward. And fast till Beelzebub and all these evils depart from you and all the angels of our earthly mother come and serve you. For I tell you truly unless you fast you shall never be free from the power of Satan and from all diseases that come from Satan. Fast and pray fervently seeking the power of the living God for your healing. While you fast, eschew the sins of man and seek our earthly mothers angels for he that seek shall find.

Seek the fresh air of the forest and of the fields and there in the midst of them shall you find the angel of air. Pull off your shoes and your clothing and suffer the angel of air to embrace all your body. Then breathe long and deeply that the angel of air may be brought within you. I tell you truly the angel of air shall cast out of your body all uncleanness, which defiled it without and within. And thus shall all evil smelling and unclean things rise out of you as the smoke of fire curls upwards and is lost in the sea of the air. For I tell you truly holy is the angel of air who cleanses all that is unclean and makes all evil smelling things of a sweet, sweet odor. No man may come before the face of God who the angel of air lets not pass. Truly, truly all must be born again by air and by truth for your body breathes the air of the earthly mother and your spirit breathes the truth of the heavenly father.

After the angel of air, seek the angel of water. Put off your shoes and your clothing and suffer the angel of water to embrace all your body. Cast yourself wholly into his enfolding arms and as often as you move the air with your breath, move with your body the water also. I tell you truly the angel of water shall cast out of your body all uncleanness, which defiled you without and within. And all unclean and evil smelling things shall flow out of you as the uncleanness of garments washed in water flow away and are lost in the stream of the river. I tell you truly holy is the angel of water who cleanses all that is unclean and makes all evil smelling things of a sweet odor. No man may come before the face of God whom the angel of water lets not pass. In your truth all must be born again of water and of truth. Your body bathes in the river of earthly life and your spirit bathes in the river of earthly life and your spirit bathes in the river of life everlasting. For you receive your blood from our earthly mother and the truth from our heavenly father think not that it is sufficient that the angel of water embrace you outwards only. I tell you truly the uncleanness within is greater by much than the uncleanness without. And he who cleanses himself without but within remains unclean is like two tones that outward are painted fair but are within full of all of uncleanness and abominations so I tell you truly suffer the angel of water to baptize you also within that you may become free from all your past sins and that within likewise you may become as pure as the rivers foam scorching in the sunlight.

Seek therefore a large trailing gourd having a stalk the length of a man. Take out its inwards and fill it with water from the river, which the sun has warmed. Hang it upon the branch of a tree and kneel upon the ground before the angel of water and suffer the end of the stalk of the trailing gourd to enter your hinder parts that the water may flow through all your bowels. Afterwards, rest kneeling on the ground before the angel of water and pray to the living God that he will forgive you all your past sins and pray the angel of water that he will free your body from every uncleanness and disease. Then let the water run out from your body that it may carry away from within it all the unclean and evil smelling things of Satan, and you shall see with your eyes and smell with your nose all the abominations and uncleanness which defiled the temple of your body. Even all the sins, which abide in your body tormenting you with all manner of pains. I tell you truly baptism with water frees you from all of these. Renew your baptizing with water on every day of your fast until the day when you see that the water, which flows out of you, is as pure as the river's foam. Then take your body to the coursing river and there in the arms of the angel of water render thanks to the living God that he has freed you from your sins. And this holy baptizing by the angel of water is rebirth unto the new life. For your eyes shall henceforth see and your ears shall hear. Sin no more therefore after your baptism that the angels of air and of water may eternally abide in you and serve you evermore.

CHAPTER 1

Free Will

If God, the Creator, respects our free will, then so should mankind. As a society, we need to remain free to choose our methods and modalities of health care. If our freedom of choice is ever removed, then we will be forced into illness, because freedom and health go hand in hand. This is a universal truth, one the very Creator abides by.

God has revealed that our responsibility is to be a good steward of our bodies. The Dead Sea Scrolls explain how to clean our bowel with water in order to pull all manner of disease from our bodies. If we become ill, God has provided the information as to how and what to do. I have known many wonderful people who became ill early in life and asked God to heal them, perhaps they misunderstood the answer they received. God will not violate his own word, but if we are not good stewards of our bodies, then we face our own consequences. God's will is that we receive what we want, wellness or sickness, both by our own hand. Therefore it cannot be fair to blame him and say that illness is what God wanted for us! If we have not obtained the full reward, we have stayed shortsighted and have not evolved our thought processes and actions into God's. God is the master he created health and wellness.

CHAPTER 2

The Soul

"The physical body provides a point of focus on the earth through which the soul can experience life. It is a means for the soul to enter school to learn an entirely new set of lessons, which can greatly accelerate spiritual growth.

We must learn to treat the physical body as the Divine being and partner that it is. It has intelligence and can communicate. It desires to be of service to the Divine plan and us as long as we will give it the respect of an equal partner.

The four bodies are like musical instruments, each with a different vibration and tone. We must learn to weave these bodies together into a beautiful symphony. To always play just one instrument would be boring or monotonous. To play them all together in perfect balance and harmony, in service of the soul and God's Divine plan, is what the Masters have referred to as 'the music of the spheres...'"

This beautiful information comes from Joshua David Stone, Ph.D., author of *Soul Psychology*. His analogy of the four bodies is simply splendid. His teachings are healing and will help us throughout our lifetimes to evolve, just a he says.

It is very clear to me that my mission is to teach my fellow human beings the "how to" or the practical application of valuable principles that will enhance the quality of their lives, specifically, with the physical body and colon hygiene. I personally have to do all the work necessary at all levels to evolve in the emotional, mental, and spiritual bodies.

I have to admit that it has been a very challenging task to motivate individuals to do their physical plane work, especially at the bowel management level. It is easier to have massages, oil baths, take a supplement, read a book, have emotional work done, or be in a more passive posture in pursuit of your health care than to get up on the table and have to really look at the horrifying abominations that are coming out of YOUR body. There is totally and absolutely no one else you can blame for this horrible negligence and abuse, but yourself! I guess that is why colonics are not the most popular modality! That is why we must submit ourselves to God's truths in order to obtain the full reward. Remember, the Dead Sea Scrolls state that all manner of disease comes out through the bowel, the abominations will come out through the bowel, and the abominations WITHIN are greater than the abominations without! So let's not fool ourselves! Actually if you think about it, God has a hysterical sense of humor! We are all on the same level playing field. He is no respector of persons! God's idea of obtaining humility is probably quite different than what we may have imagined. Also, I promise you, that as you witness these phenomena of abominations, you will never look at another human being again and think that you are better than they are.

It doesn't matter what your name is, how much money you make, or where you came from (actually we all came from the same place). You still have to remove the environmental pollutants just like everyone else and in the same manner, if you want true vitality and health. The same work is required by all. Only the negative ego will try to stop you. We all have to look at our own "CRAP" in order to get healed whether we like it or not! The real question is "When?" "GROSS DENIAL COULD BE A VERY HARMFUL WEAPON WE USE UPON OURSELVES AS A NATION." In other words, "what you don't know could (very most definitely) hurt you."

CHAPTER 3

Poverty Consciousness

Poverty consciousness is a very destructive thought process. This consciousness came into existence in full force during and as a result of the Depression. America lived a simple and principally based existence previous to this time, which people were quite happy with. As the Depression decade was released upon the American people, it literally tore the first and second charkas of the American people apart. Just as it did to the American Indians when they were forced off their land and homes into reservations. And just like it did to the German population at the end of the First World War.

When the first and second charkas are traumatized, this violation to self-esteem is so fractured that the individual will do and take almost anything presented to them to ease their pain. This is the violation that is present with alcoholism, drug addiction, and any other addiction. But it can be healed when the traumas are released as the individual does his work by seeking out the emotional healer familiar with this kind of work.

By the end of the 1930's, the American people were so broken down that they were ready to believe anything. New ideas were presented to them about health care and the principally based basic health care procedures were traded in. Today we are witnessing how these complicated and greed-based practices are faltering.

Now, remember that curses or thought processes are passed down from generation to generation. If broken charkas are not healed, children will continue to live in the same fear-based realities as their parents, who actually experienced the initial situation.

Germany allowed Hitler to come in slowly as he promised to rebuild and restructure a broken nation. Little did the people of Germany know that they had sold their broken soul for this man's ego, greed, and his very hidden agenda. Finally, a decade later they saw the total destruction of their country again because they had allowed themselves to be controlled by this egomaniac.

Being responsible for each decision that you can make every day is a high calling and one the CREATOR has given to you solely. Your choice does make a mark on your own life and the life of your country. Please take it seriously and hold others accountable for this also: your teachers, your political figures, your church elders, your doctors and health care practitioners, your friends and your family.

Do not let the illusion that your lifestyle cannot afford you the information and implementation of good sounding information stop you from a healthy and abundant life. Prioritize your spending. Utilize the energy used on non-profitable activity and put it into health-giving activities. The Universe will bless you and God will ALWAYS cause you to prosper when you take this action. You will be learning how to submit your ego to your higher self. YOU HOLD THE KEY TO THIS POWER!

Chapter 4

Hypothyroidism

It is my opinion that the thyroid gland is as important as the colon. If the colon is clean, it helps to provide an avenue and place for the other organs to dump their waste and thus stay functioning optimally. If the thyroid gland is healthy, then it will provide the sufficient energy flow to every organ and system, which will keep the metabolism running efficiently.

In this day and age, it is important to understand a few truths. First, there are only a few foods that feed the thyroid gland. They are bladder wrack, Irish moss, kelp, fish, and dulce. Now, how many times in your life have you eaten those foods? As a society, our thyroids are undernourished. Secondly, we have to bring into this equation the truth that we as a nation are living with large quantities of heavy metals. They will infiltrate the body at all levels, and predominantly settle in the weak areas throughout the body including the thyroid. Thirdly, we have to bring into this equation the truth that we as a nation have had to deal with generational disorders concerning shame and guilt. The thyroid gland is located in the 5th charka, so it is a perfect place to house emotional traumas. From here we speak and say what we feel. But we have been told over and over again, "Don't say that; don't tell the truth because it cannot be received," or simply "Be quiet; shut up; shhhhhh!" So we have shut off the flow of energy emotionally at the important juncture relied upon for energy distribution.

Remember that the thyroid gland controls the basal metabolic rate for the whole body. I have met very few people with an optimally functioning thyroid; the exception being those who understand these truths and have done the necessary work to resolve and heal the situation.

Some of you are sitting there saying, "I have had my thyroid tested by my doctor and it works just fine." Many of my clients have also made that statement, however, because they have taken the proper steps to heal their thyroid gland, they are much healthier and happier. When you do the right things you get the obvious results. You have genuine energy.

Dr. Arnold J. Susser, R.P., Ph.D., creator of state-of-the-art nutritional supplements for over twenty years, states "Many experts maintain that regular laboratory tests are not adequate predictors of the true state of the thyroid. In addition, standard thyroid tests do not isolate the active thyroid hormones, T4 and T3."

After initially using organic iodine, atomidine, from Edgar Casey's information, I switched over to a product named METABO-RIGHT. I felt this product addressed and supported the health aspects of the entire thyroid gland. This is the product designed by Dr. Susser. I felt sure this product was a thorough source of nutrition for a human body and have taken it daily for six years.

Many people have chosen to take this product over the years. My observations are that this is a very necessary food for people who would like to restore the full function of their thyroid gland. I have two case histories to share in support of this observation.

Two female clients decided to do a series of colonics. One was 22 years old; the other was 37 years old. The younger woman had not had her period in five months. The older woman had not had her period for seven years. After ten colonics and ten days of Metabo-Right, the younger woman started her period again as normal. After thirteen days of colonics and taking Metabo-Right, the older woman also started her period. If the thyroid is responsible for the functioning of hormones, then it makes sense to begin with the thyroid when ruling out various causes of hormonal health issues? I have witnessed improvements like these consistently.

When the thyroid gland is supported, mild cases of depression have improved. This is because the thyroid oversees the energy input to the master organ of the endocrine system, the pituitary gland. The result is mental clarity and vibrancy.

If an individual is in a major health crisis, he or she will always muscle test for glandulars. Health requires that the basic energetic system functions and the main control tower here is the thyroid gland.

There are major differences between synthetic drugs and organic products. Synthetic drugs are produced artificially by man in a laboratory. Organic products have been created by God Almighty. You choose! I know countless clients who have chosen the synthetic route; some who have taken it over twenty years and their thyroid still does not function properly as they display symptoms of hypothyroidism. Doctors switch and change the synthetic medications in hopes of correcting the problem to no avail.

Notice that the entire make-up of the body, with the exception of the blood, is fed by foods that are predominantly exclusive to feeding the thyroid. The structure of the body is made-up largely by calcium phosphate (57%), calcium carbonate (10%), and magnesium phosphate (1.3%).

These same components can be found in certain herbs and foods. For example, the brain and nerves are maintained by potassium and magnesium phosphate, also found in lady slipper, Irish moss, kelp, gotu kola and ginseng. The connective tissue is made up of silica, also found in Irish moss, shave grass, and kelp. The muscles use magnesium, potassium and calcium phosphates and chlorides found in these same foods as well as bladder wrack, flaxseed meal, comfrey, and elderberry.

Interestingly, the bones are made up of calcium and calcium fluoride. We know that osteoporosis is caused from a lack of calcium, but as many Americans beef up on calcium supplements, bone spurs and calcium deposits occur causing great harm. It is possible that calcium itself is not the problem, but that we are not assimilating the calcium because the thyroid lacks energy to stimulate the parathyroid glands. These bean-shaped glands near the lateral thyroid lobes control the amounts of calcium in the blood.

In 1996 I personally experienced a skeletal breakdown. Simply by feeding and healing my thyroid gland, I regenerated my bones without the use of any calcium supplements. I would propose that osteoporosis is directly related to a poorly functioning thyroid gland.

CHAPTER 5

The Full Circle of Healing

An important key leading to full vitality is to discover the necessary steps to recover health. Chelation therapy is a useful tool that allows various naturally occurring substances to enter the bloodstream by IV into a vein at the elbow. Poisons, pollution, and parasites are cleansed from the tissue and organs and are dumped into the kidneys. Chelation is fabulous for cleaning the artery walls and the entire vascular system. Isn't it thrilling to know that a loved one does not have to have their chest cavity sawed wide open, but instead can have this procedure done!

If you are having chelation therapy on a regular basis, you will see obvious improvement over time. However, as the blood passes through the body at all levels, it becomes repolluted—within 24 hours. It's like treading water. A person's health may not progress negatively, but the improvement can only go so far. The initial cause for disease still remains. The bowel is so full of old diseased feces that they continuously repollute the body.

Repollution is why you may see someone doing chelation therapy and they feel at least happy to be alive, but you will not see much outward physical change. If you do chelation therapy and systematic bowel management in order to pull out large amounts of waste collected by the chelation, you will see the internal health situation change, and flow over into the wonderful external manifestation of vitality and health.

So my question is this: How many pieces of the health puzzle to you want? My personal prayer has been—I want it all—and will do whatever work is required to obtain the total results!

CHAPTER 6

The Great Discrepancy

I would like to discuss the subject of X-raying the wonderful colon and the usefulness of the colonoscopy procedure.

The question most asked of me is: "How can so many feces pass through the tube during a colonic when my colonoscopy showed that my bowel is clean?" Well, I do not understand this discrepancy. All I know is what I see with my own eyes and what the client sees also!

A man in his seventies scheduled a series of fifteen colonics. He had been active and vital his entire life, but he started experiencing tremors. He was scheduled for a colonoscopy and came to see me first.

Each day this man not only released large quantities through the tube, but also it came out around the scope and onto the table. With rare exception, I had never seen this happen, especially not for fifteen days straight! Since he had been in the construction business and familiar with measurement, I asked him how much he thought the feces weighed from each colonic. He told me that easily it would amount to seven pounds. That's seven pounds every day for fifteen days.

Now he went for his colonoscopy. The results were that his colon was clean.

This gentleman came back for another series and for fifteen days he again released in the same manner as with the first series. We saw so much poop that I set my garbage can next to my table and threw away the soiled towels each day. The man could not believe what he was witnessing. So he asked, "How could so much poop be coming out of me when my test results showed that my colon is clean?" All I could say was, "I don't know, but let's pack up this poop into a bucket and take it to your doctor and ask him!" One thing I am certain is that the truth always reveals itself in time.

The second case history I would like to share with you is about a woman in her mid-sixties. After recovering two years previously from lung cancer with the help of chemotherapy and radiation, she decided to do a series of fifteen colonics. For some reason, her bowel had shut down and she felt concerned and of course, uncomfortable.

She had seen her doctor about this and was given a colonoscopy. X-rays were taken of her colon. Her test results were that her colon was "clean" and that she was fine. Her doctor suggested she take Metamucil and sent her on her merry way.

The adult daughter became concerned for her mother's health and brought her to me for colonics. She still was not pooping.

Her bowel released substantial amounts during the beginning sessions and then for days simply shut off. Very little released and this client felt concerned enough to call and cancel her remaining appointments. We discussed her situation and we agreed to try it one more time. She explained that there were times she could not get off the toilet for the huge volume of feces releasing several hours straight as if a trap door were opened. Then it would close and she would not go to the bathroom for days.

During her next colonic, I decided to massage her bowel. The bowel loves this manipulation and often it helps with releasing. When I put my hand on her transverse colon at the center, I felt a ball about the size of an orange. I advised her to return to her doctor at her earliest convenience and contacted her daughter as well.

Her doctor was not the least bit concerned and even denied them another test. The daughter fought this and finally this woman was given an MRI. Sitting right in the center of her transverse colon was a tumor! Thank God it was operable and she received three more years of life.

My question is this: How accurate are these tests given to us with "wonderfully" technologically designed machines? What is the factor of human error? Sometimes the intuition of a therapist can accomplish a lot!

CHAPTER 7

Light Manifests Things in the Darkness

When utilized correctly, the modality of colonics will bring to light other dysfunctions in the organs of the body. This follows the principle that light will make manifest those things hidden in the dark.

The bowel operates by a peristaltic pump. As the bowel is cleaned, this pumping action will also stimulate other connected organs into cleansing mode. Let me give you two examples.

The kidneys can back-up with debris—we have all heard of people who have gotten kidney stones as a result. As the kidney tries to eliminate this debris, you can have tremendous pain. The peristaltic action of the colon being cleansed will trigger the kidneys to cleanse and on two occasions, my clients discovered they had stones.

Do colonics cause these stones to formulate? No, the process was in motion prior to the colonic. The colonic merely shed light on the broader health condition, so now the individual can do the right things so the full healing can occur.

You do NOT need to be afraid of colonics. "For God has not given us the spirit of fear, but of power, of love, and of a sound mind."

The next situation concerned a lovely young woman. After twenty colonics, during her sessions she would experience pain and push on the area of her female organs. I had never seen anyone behave this way. I asked her to see her doctor.

Their discovery was this: her uterus was literally housing fecal matter as a result of anal intercourse, obviously not practicing any form of hygiene. Thank God she had done colonics to spur her uterus into a cleansing mode. Otherwise she may have passed away suddenly had it gone unnoticed. But she had taken a positive direction to become well and her body displayed the right symptoms for her to then become well again.

If we practice habits of colon hygiene, even as the Creator has established, then we can become so familiar with our bodies that we catch disease at the very beginning stages. YOU hold the key to this power!

CHAPTER 8

Yeast

When I was quite ill during the late 1980's, there was little discussion on the subject of yeast. Today it is seriously addressed.

It has been demonstrated that the body produces certain substances as a protective agent, like mucous and cholesterol. Most people do not know that the bowel produces vast amounts of mucous as protection against highly processed and over-cooked foods or that the liver produces cholesterol for lubrication to protect the arteries. I believe that yeast is also used by the body to protect itself. The sword is double-edged because parasites thrive in mucous and in yeasty environments.

However, most Americans are walking around with traces of heavy metals polluting the brain, the heart and fatty tissue. As a protective measure, I believe that the body utilizes yeast as a protective agent against heavy metals. It serves as a buffer.

Heavy metals are hot to the body. Heat flashes may result as they course through the body. I personally experienced this; my feet and hands felt continuously hot as burners. The body supports yeast as long as we store heavy metals. In many ways we should be thankful for wonderful natural intelligence. To clear up the yeast, we will need to remove the cause, which are heavy metals.

Hopefully, we understand how serious this is. Many young people are suffering from strokes and heart attacks these days. I believe this is connected to the use of mercury in dental work. I have known people who have had heart attacks after having their mercury fillings removed and also after they have had traditional dental work. Unfortunately, statistics are not available until this subject is taken seriously in this country.

Mercury and silver are being released into the body cavity at the same time the dental fillings are removed and travel throughout the body and cause great harm. I exhort everyone to research and observe what they see and form their own conclusions. Natural Vegetable Glycerin works well to chelate the metals into the alimentary canal and colonics help to pull metals out from the body cavity. But this is an area where you must become an expert as you take charge of your own health care, otherwise you allow yourself to be at the mercy of others who profess to be so called experts.

CHAPTER 9

Skin Cancer

It is my belief that skin cancer is not caused by sun exposure, but from a general deterioration of our health as a culture. Within the last decade, we have added a wide variety of poisons to our lifestyle, including processed foods, dental work, and the manufacturing of skin and grooming products that contain toxins, including the use of prescription drugs.

For example, as people grow older, "age spots" are commonly accepted. This has been attributed to the deterioration of the liver; however, the liver need not deteriorate with age if we follow the appropriate cleansing laws. As the bowel becomes filthy, the liver cannot detox and dump waste into the colon. Thus you find these spots appear on the skin. These spots will disappear with aggressive bowel management as the degeneration process actually reverses with the rebuilding of the digestive system and organs.

Do not believe what the experts say about the origin of disease. They may not be anywhere near accurate! We are led to believe that cancer is genetic, but then cancers affect whole neighborhoods near chemical plants. And you will discover that many of the recipients of skin cancer have not even been exposed to the sun.

You hold the key to your own power of health. Do not be like the children of Israel who were lost in the wilderness for 40 years. They spent this time roaming within an eleven-mile radius. How is that for relying on man's expertise!

CHAPTER 10

The Victim Mentality

Victim mentality has permeated our culture. You've heard it: "I don't have time or the money; If this was God's will we would already be doing it in the medical field; my doctor doesn't support this; my family and friends don't support this; I'm too afraid."

God has laid the details out for those who are brave and will do their own work. "The thief cometh not, but for to steal, kill, and destroy, but I am come that they might have life and have it more abundantly." As we implement steps toward securing our health, we must take deliberate action to clean our body cavities, eat healthy, and support our emotional healing. As we demonstrate action lined-up with God's words, we will reap those blessings. We otherwise are easily manipulated and controlled.

CHAPTER 11

Curing the Common Cold

Why would you want to cure the common cold? Why would anyone in his or her right mind want to stop the state of the art detoxing mechanism that has been Divinely constructed? When the body is under attack from various germs, it responds with a cleansing mode unequaled to rid the body of those germs. The nose may run and the sinus cavities release fluids to push bacteria out, but this is just the system working efficiently so that vitality can return.

So what if you are under the weather for a few days! Embrace it; take the time to regenerate, as the time for rest is essential. The only time the human body stops detoxing is when it is dead. We have already blocked the bowel from detoxing and if we stop the sinuses from releasing, we may just blow up!

If you do not allow the body to develop a fever and detox, especially when young, you remain unhealthy and vulnerable during your entire life. If you take synthetic medicines, you might stop the temporary symptoms, but the inevitable has merely been postponed. After enough postponements you may watch the surfacing of these dormant causes develop as a serious illness down the road. The sooner the initial cause is removed, the faster the body recuperates. Longevity and quality of life are enhanced. Each time the immune system is compromised with the use of a drug, instead of allowing the fever and detox, so is quality and longevity of that life.

Foreigners frequently ask me why we have so many drug stores in America. We have forgotten that we have an optimally efficient body made by the Creator. When you get a cold, stay home and rest. That may be the cure. And it is a very good thing when the human body comes down with a cold or the flu.

CHAPTER 12

Reprint of V.E. Irons

The following was written by Victor Earl Irons, a health care practitioner working during the last century. This small brochure was found in a box in my garage in 1994. Where it came from, I do not know. It was tattered and torn and probably no longer in print. The title: "The Destruction of Your Own Natural Protective Mechanism."

We appreciate this man's contribution toward truth as his words turn out to be a tremendous blessing and a powerful message. May we have the wisdom to love ourselves enough, in order to do the fundamental work required, that we might live abundantly during our stay here on Earth. The brochure is reprinted in its entirety.

"Many letters are received daily in which the writer carefully catalogues all their ailments and health history. But I think it is only fair to tell you that I am not a medical doctor and don't believe in all the theories and propaganda this country has had to absorb regarding disease.

I especially do not believe in the whole concept that we are taught and that you and your neighbors believe, namely, that each individual is different from another; that what is one man's medicine is another man's poison—ALL this propaganda may be true as to drugs, but not as far as NATURAL HEALTH is concerned. I believe that the CREATOR made us all alike and that what is good for one health wise is good for everyone. I appreciate the fact that this is considered heresy by the medical profession, yet you and the rest of the United States have been suffering new types of disease every day for years, so that apparently the whole concept under which we are living is WRONG.

Let us withdraw ourselves from the earth and get above it so that we can see the whole in perspective:

In 1900 the United States was the healthiest of all 93 civilized countries. We were a young, vibrant, healthy people. To be sure, we then had all types of diseases, which killed off 29 babies out of every hundred the first year. Back then, in ages from one to fifteen years, contagious diseases took enormous toll bringing the life span way down, but the same was true of all other nations. However, those who did make it to 15 years of age had a far better chance of living a healthful life to a ripe old age than any of us have today.

By 1920, the United States had dropped to SECOND place of 93 nations.

In 1978 the U.S. Public Health Service, which at that time told the truth, claimed that we had dropped to 79th place. Today, at the same rate, we would land somewhere in 92nd or 93rd place. The rate of deterioration has been so rapid that the U.S. Public Health Service apparently now controlled by the same clique that has caused the deterioration, will no longer give us the true facts. But, back then we still had the truth.

In 1900 when as a nation we were at our peak in health, we lived under different theories and concepts regarding health and disease than we do today. Back then we had some very brilliant doctors. Some 80 years ago, Dr. Oliver Wendell Holmes told us that if all the medical material were dumped into the sea, it would be all the better for mankind and all the worse for the fishes. Dr. J.H. Tilden of Denver, Colorado at that time specialized in pneumonia which was then the #1 killer. He had more pneumonia cases than any other doctor for which there was any record and he never lost a patient. WHY? He used NO DRUGS whatsoever, just cleaned out the colon, water therapy, fasting, and natural live foods, etc.

At the turn of the century (1900), the Mayo brothers in Rochester, Minnesota built a reputation under which the doctors have been thriving on for over 80 years. Thirty years ago, I personally met a nurse who worked with Charles Mayo for 15 years before he died. She said that Dr. Charles would start visiting his patients at 7am. He stuffed the right side of all his pockets with raisins and the left side with nuts and kept going until seven in the evening munching on nothing but nuts and raisins, using NO DRUGS and NO "DEAD" foods.

Dr. Mayo made this statement for public consumption: "We are all afraid of germs because we are all ignorant of them. Germs are outside. What we should be afraid of is lowered resistance, which comes from within. The folly of our topsy-turvy notion leads to much preventable confusion and despair. Instead of developing a proper respect for our own extraordinary powers, conferred upon us by Mother Nature, we endow germs with unnatural powers, which they should not possess. Here let me repeat one solemn truth, which should be repeated over and over each day until everybody comprehends it's meaning and acts upon it. NORMAL RESISTANCE TO DISEASE IS DIRECTLY DEPENDENT UPON ADEQUATE FOOD. NORMAL RESISTANCE TO DISEASE NEVER COMES OUT OF PILL BOXES. ADEQUATE FOOD IS THE CRADLE OF NORMAL RESISTANCE, THE PLAYGROUND OF NORMAL IMMUNITY, THE WORKSHOP OF GOOD HEALTH AND THE LABORATORY OF LONG LIFE." *Dr. Charles Mayo*

Also, in 1900, Boston had seven of the leading doctors in the country, so that people were attracted from all over the world. None of those seven doctors used drugs. I personally knew one of them a short time before he too died. The type of therapy that predominates at any given time reflects the health of a nation at that time. Above I have given you the type, which prevailed from 1870 to 1915 when we were at our HEALTH ZENITH—NO DRUGS.

In 1935, at 40 years of age, this writer's doctor in Boston did his best for three years to keep my sacroiliac in place. (In the sacroiliac you have something similar to a ball in a socket. If the socket fills up with unassimilated calcium, the ball can easily be crowded out. If it is out as much as 1/4" the ligaments are stretched and the pain is like a sprained ankle.)

The first year I went to see my doctor about once a month. The second, three times a month, and the third year, I would have liked to have seen him three times a day because my sacroiliac would come out with the slightest motion causing tremendous pain. Finally he told me that he would take NO more of my MONEY, but he did request that for my own benefit, and his own peace of mind, I go immediately to the hospital and get X-rays of my entire spinal column from the back of the head to the coccyx. This I did. Several weeks later, he called me to his office and showed me the X-rays of the spinal column and each individual vertebra thereof. Then he told me that he had submitted the X-rays to three of the leading surgeons in Boston and to one other osteopath physician. None of the doctors knew that he had showed the X-rays to anyone else. In every case, each doctor diagnosed it as "MARIE STRUEMPELL ARTHRITIS" for which they claim there is no cure: Today it is called "ANKYLOSING SPONDYLOSIS." This disease is an arthritic condition where the calcium is not assimilated and builds calcium spurs in exactly the same relative position on every vertebra and all about the same sized spurs so that eventually, as these spurs grow, the patient begins to stoop imperceptibly, but within 20 years, the body is doubled over so that the head is below the knee, but you can still walk.

I had read a little on NATURAL METHODS of healing and replied to my doctor—"I do not believe that there is any such thing as an INCURABLE DISEASE, but I admit there are millions of incurable people." "But," I continued, "Doc, I want to thank you for bringing this to my attention—it gives me something new to live for, but you can rest assured, that I have no intention of being numbered with the MILLIONS OF INCURABLES." WITHIN TWO MONTHS, I HAD NO MORE PAIN FROM DISPLACEMENT AND WITHIN 14 MONTHS PRACTICALLY NO SPURS—ALL DONE WITH CLEANSING, FASTING AND NATURAL FOODS AND WITHOUT DRUGS.

From that time to the present, my whole theory of LIFE and DISEASE is: "THERE IS ONLY ONE GOD, THERE IS ONLY ONE SUPREME POWER, THERE IS ONLY ONE CAUSE OF DISEASE, THERE IS ONLY ONE DISEASE, AND THEREFORE, THERE IS ONLY ONE TREATMENT FOR ALL DISEASE." For the last 47 years in my lectures and with knowledge concerning hundreds of thousands of people, I have never found the slightest reason to change my thinking.

Of course, this is all medical heresy in this country and I paid the penalty they demanded. In 1956, I was hauled into Federal Court in Boston, Mass., and found guilty on SIX counts, fined $2,000.00 on each count, ($1,000.00 on each count for myself and $1,000 on each for my companies) making a total of $12,000.00 and ONE year in jail. It should be noted, however, that these charges were only MISDEMEANORS and NOT FELONIES. Misdemeanors are such things as spitting on the sidewalk, speeding, running through a red light or failing to stop at a stop sign.

At that time, back in 1956, you seldom got a fine over $25.00 to $100.00 for any of these misdemeanors, even for a second or third offense. Even the attorneys for the FDA thought this was a pretty steep sentence. A jail sentence for a misdemeanor was seldom if ever heard of. So, before I got out of the courthouse, the government attorneys told my attorney that if I would sign the CONSENT DECREE, which had been signed by all of my competitors, they would not prosecute (to abandon) the whole deal. I happen to have read and studied that CONSENT DECREE and so I quickly told my attorney to inform the government attorneys that I would see them all in HELL before I would sign my name to 57 innuendoes, lies, and falsehoods.

Within half an hour, my attorney was back with a new proposal that if I would go out of business, they would not prosecute the whole matter. I replied that I had done nothing wrong and that I was being prosecuted simply because my teachings of the TRUTH hurt big business. So, I paid the $12,000.00 fine and assumed my debt to society by going to Federal Penitentiary, serving five months and two days.

Meantime, everything I had predicted would happen to our national health has happened and with a vengeance. Even President Johnson himself repeated my exact warning except for two words. I had claimed that the ENTIRE COUNTRY was suffering from deficiency disease due to— The late President Johnson said that substantial segments of the country were suffering from deficiency disease due to— TIME has proven that the ENTIRE COUNTRY has rapidly deteriorated and I challenge the world that you couldn't find in the USA, 1,000 people who don't have a clogged colon. Just let me get them on a COLEMA BOARD and on the 7 day Cleansing Program both at the same time and we will show any challengers WHAT WE MEAN. We will let them see, feel, and even hold in their hands exactly what has been thickening, hardening, and decaying in their colon for years, causing all types of dies-ease (lack of ease).

The condition of the colons in this entire country are FAR WORSE than either the doctors, the AMA, the drug houses, the Chemical industry, the Food processors, the President, the Congress, the Supreme Court or even the Natural Health Industry have any conception.

Our first hand knowledge obtained by the use of the 7 Day Cleansing Program with the Colema Board amazed even us. Most colons today are all so badly distorted we can't believe what we see. It is probably too late to save our Nation, but we CAN SAVE thousands of individuals who can see, and believe in our theory that the CAUSE OF MOST CONDITIONS OF ILL HEALTH IS AUTO-INTOXIFICATION and that 95% of their troubles start in the colon.

We can prove that we can find hardened mucous with its foul smelling curd in the colons of 95% of the entire nation.

HOW DO WE KNOW THIS? Because possibly 99% of all ages and sexes have violated two of the major natural laws from one to three times every day since they were two years old. What are these two laws?

1. The WRONG combination of foods.

2. The constant daily use of tremendous amounts of DEAD FOOD.

The wrong application of both of these laws has caused the body's natural protective mechanism to secrete mucous into the colon to protect the body from absorbing the many poisons that those counterfeit foods create. But we have simply OVERWORKED Nature's protective mechanism to the point that the mechanism, instead of protecting us from our poisons, now itself poisons us.

You see, Nature's protective mechanism was not designed for the enormous and continuous use to which it has been subjected to protect us from the occasional ingestion of poisonous food that ordinarily might happen only once or twice a month or less. When food that is NOT WHOLESOME or is HARMFUL to the body reaches the stomach, word is immediately sent from the stomach to the mucous manufacturer warning: "Get busy, the enemy is on the way." The way in which the message is sent is immaterial. WE DO KNOW THAT MUCOUS STARTS TO BE PRODUCED IMMEDIATLY AND THE COLON IS LINED WITH IT. Twelve to 18 hours later when the poisoned or harmful food from the stomach finally enters the colon, the latter is well prepared with a layer of mucous lining it so the body does not absorb any of the poison. Were this to happen once or even several times a month, this mucous, having been used would disintegrate and slowly be discharged from the colon with no harm done. But it is now certainly apparent that NATURE never intended that this protective mechanism would be used as continuously as it is today. This protective mechanism was never designed to continue secreting mucous one layer on top of another layer for years with no time out or chance for its elimination. The result is that layer on top of layer is secreted until its accumulation thickens to 1/8" to 1/4" thick. Sometimes this layer or layers gets to 3/8" to 1/2" in thickness, becoming as hard and black as a piece of old hardened rubber you see on a highway from a truck tire. It cannot be cut with a knife, but you can cut it with a razor blade. Usually it breaks into innumerable small pieces. But we have had specimens saved in alcohol from several inches to a few feet in length while the longest we have had was 27 ft. (in one piece). Sometimes it will come out as a pile weighing as much as 11 lbs. and continuing to come out for several days to a week. The 7 day cleansing program loosens this debris, and by using the Colema Board it is all collected in a colander, like the one you use in your kitchen. Place the colander in the toilet. Thus all that comes out of you will dump into the colander. The fecal matter will go through the colander, but the hardened mucous will not. When all the water has run through you, get up, flush the toilet, take out the colander and put it under the faucet until this hardened mucous is relatively clean. Then dump it out on a white paper towel or paper plate and examine it. You will see it as a series of inner tubes within each other. You can see, feel, examine and handle this accumulation with your own fingers. You suddenly realize that you are holding in your hands the very material that can and may have caused all your aches, pains, and symptoms—some of which may have been given a scientific name denoting a serious condition of ill health. What you are seeing is the end result of self-made toxins. Since you are taking two Colemas a day, this means it is the eighth or ninth Colema before the old hardened accumulated mucous, so tightly imbedded in the colon for months or years, comes out. It has probably been slowly emitting poisons into your bloodstream, causing all types of distorted symptoms. Once this hardened mucous starts to eliminate, it will be trapped in the colander so that you can wash it and examine it. If it is still coming out at the end of the 7th day, continue the program for another 2 or 3 days or until there is no more coming out.

Anyone who disagrees with any of the above—REMEMBER, you CAN PROVE it to your own satisfaction by what comes from your own body for the smallest conceivable investment. There is no substitute for experience, and we challenge EVERYONE to experience this for themselves.

It is horrible to realize how we ABUSE NATURE'S protective mechanism, destroying it to the point where IT ITSELF becomes toxic and is a continuous disease producer. To be sure, the waste product of normal metabolism is toxic and the only reason we are not poisoned by it is because it is removed from the body as fast as it is produced. But this is not the case with this hardened mucous—it is NOT REMOVED but lies imbedded in the vast folds of the colon continuously emitting toxins—TOXEMIA—AUTOINTOXIFICATION—the primary cause of most disease.

We are NOT exaggerating nor bluffing. Regardless of your financial standing, regardless of your past health history, regardless of your age (over two years), or sex, YOU (meaning the reader and 95% of the USA) DO HAVE THIS HARDENED MUCOUS IN YOUR COLON AND YOU WILL BE AMAZED AT WHAT COMES OUT OF YOU.

Isn't it about time you really know what is happening in your body????"

Chapter 13

An Arm and a Leg

I have dropped forty pounds in the last year. I used no synthetics. I did not participate in any weight loss program. Through cleansing, the return of vitality simply regenerated my body. Anybody can achieve the same result and it won't cost an arm and a leg!

My weight gain was associated with the removal of my mercury dental fillings. I understood the importance of detoxing heavy metals from my system. For this I used Natural Vegetable Glycerin—any brand will suffice. It's cheap. I simultaneously took a product called KANTITA, from Kroeger Herb, Inc. for yeast removal. As the heavy metals and the yeast came out from my body cavity, I also shed unwanted pounds.

Of course, colonics during this process cannot be substituted. There is no placebo affect when it comes to instilling real vitality and health!

This process does not require a lot of expense, despite that there are those who would have you believe otherwise. Chelation therapy is popular and costly. Yet I accomplished the same result without one chelation treatment. You can do things for yourself that a supplement company can never do for you!

If you cannot afford to install a colonics unit, Colema Boards are inexpensive. No one can ever stop you from getting healed in the privacy of your own home. The Creator designed our bodies in the manner such that we have the tools and means to heal ourselves within our daily routines. As far back as the DEAD SEA SCROLLS we are told how to do it— "Go down to the river and clean your bowel."

Never allow another human being to be in charge of your health care! Neither make the excuse that you cannot afford what it costs to feel great and vital.

CHAPTER 14

The One and Only Colonic

A male client in his late twenties came to me. He was over six feet tall and aside from one problem, he was otherwise in good health. The problem was that he hadn't had a bowel movement in over two weeks.

He had gone to a doctor, but he was told it was normal to not have a bowel movement for 18 days. The doctor suggested that he may be depressed and needed Prozac. He was under a lot of pressure having several children, several ex-wives, and several businesses.

He was not stupid. He told me that he ate a sub sandwich almost every day. That alone was about a foot long and he wondered, "Where was that going, if not *out* my body?" His spirit knew he desperately needed to go to the bathroom and that Prozac was not the answer.

During his colonic, as his bowel released, it caused his neurotransmitters to release. His legs shook and tears streamed down his face. You see, everything is connected to the bowel. For five full tanks of water, his body released huge amounts of toxins contained in his fecal matter. You never stop this intelligence until it is complete.

After this gentleman was dressed, he said, "After weeks of agony, no one knew what to do for me; but you knew exactly!" With that he picked me up two feet off the floor, hugging me and was still crying.

How did I know? I know our bodies are wonderfully formed and we are given the privilege and responsibility to be good stewards on a daily basis. The correct information always provides profitable results!

CHAPTER 15

The Unique Tool That Measures

Hanna Kroeger was born during the early 1900's to a missionary family committed to God. Her life and ministry has been a beacon of light for us all. The following information is taken from her book, "The Pendulum, The Bible, and Your Survival."

"Knowingly or unknowingly, everyone has a sixth sense. It is more developed in some than in others. Children have it more than adults and old folks often regain the ability of their childhood knowledge pertaining to the sixth sense.

Every one of our five senses can be used constructively or destructively. There are people who only see and hear evil and others who never see the snakes and beetles. They are absorbed in the beauty of a rose and do not feel the sting of the thorns.

There are people who feel gloomy all day long and others feel the sunshine on their skin and absorb it.

So it is with the sixth sense. Just invite the cleanest consciousness with the sixth sense. Christ said, "I stand at the door and knock." Please use this sixth sense to open the door for Him!

We are coming from many walks of life; we are drawn together under the banner of the Light Bearers of the Aquarian Age.

Like every student in a university, we have to work hard and diligently to learn the lessons given to us. So learn to use them in the spirit of this university and in the spirit of its President.

The first time I learned about the pendulum was through Linda Clark, famous author on nutrition. In her book, "Get Well Naturally", she describes how her friends used the pendulum, and there is where it all started for me. I took my wedding ring and hung it on a thread, dangling it over my hands, my knees and my food and, sure enough, slowly, slowly the ring started gyrating. I steadied myself in every way possible, but the ring was moving.

For one year I worked on this phenomenon, not showing it to anyone but my closest friends. I ordered books printed in England, France, and America. I found writings in the Bible about it. I talked to prominent women, to doctors, to psychologists, but no one could give me the answers I was searching for. Why does the pendulum work? Which energies are involved? There were many more questions.

Then one day—it was a marvelous spring day—I was going over some flowers, just budding close to the ground. I checked them with the pendulum to find out what rate of vibration the petals, the leaves and the roots had, when suddenly in all the peace and sunshine I felt as if a hand lay on mine and the words came to my mind. 'Let go and let God.' I relaxed; I went into my innermost and at once the pendulum gyrated differently, accurately, exactly. I found the key: "Let go and let God," and I have followed this advice since. Many are using a rod, a reed, or a stick as it is advised in the Bible. Others sit in front of a candle and, surprisingly enough, the flame answers their questions by bending forward, sideward, backward and by twisting or shaking one way or another. The American Indians find their herbal remedies with their sacred stick. We visited the Sioux Indians and graciously they invited us to take part in their herb hunting.

The rod, the reed and the staff are mentioned many times in the Bible. It was used extensively in those days to guide and measure, to bring water (Moses) and to lead the nations. The Pharaohs used it (Exodus 7:8-25). Maybe Moses learned the use of the rod from them. Among the Pharaohs this secret was very much guarded. The oldest known picture of dowsing was found in the ruins of Mesopotamia (1300 B.C.) where a priest is pictured using a forked divining rod. During the Dark Ages the use of the rod or pendulum fell in disrespect because the churches and their leaders had a funny idea to suppress their subjects and members rather than to help them. The use of the pendulum and the rod has its resurrection now. We have to turn back to the days of old to survive.

We cannot send every apple into the laboratories to find out if it is DDT drenched or arsenic sprayed or both, but we can apply the art of using the pendulum the right way to find out if the apple is poisoned or fit to eat. We cannot send every piece of meat to an inspector to find out whether or not it has trichinae or hormone residue. But we can use our pendulum to find out if the meat is good for use or not. By the way, for years Cal-Tech was teaching the use of the pendulum to especially bright and interested graduate students. So let's join the smart and intelligent crowd and use the pendulum.

Everything is vibration. Every star, every root, every flower, every seed has it's own electromagnetic charge and gives it off, spends it freely.

Jesus said, "You do not live from bread alone." Finally we catch on. Jesus forgive us that it took us so long to understand your words. It took us 2,000 years to realize how these divine force fields carry us, nourish us and keep us going. Einstein said, "energy and matter are interchangeable." The unseen energies move the rod, the reed, the pendulum. Now it is up to us to read and translate these energies correctly and only you who are founded in God's faith will do a good job.

The pendulum is not a toy and not a means for predictions. It is an instrument for your survival. In this polluted world we have to have something to measure with. In the Bible it said measure "as in the days of old."

Every head of a household, man or woman, should be using this means of measurement to guide the family safely through the labyrinth of mistakes and dark forces."

CHAPTER 16

The Reed

Recorded in the Dead Sea Scrolls is God's instruction about the use of "the reed" for removing all manner of disease through the bowel. We are told to continue the process until the water runs clean. The reed (or measuring tool) will show you when the body is cleansed and then, and not before, you will have an accurate account.

First, you must discover what it means to yourself simply by obeying this instruction. Generally, you can count on needing fifteen colonics for each year of your life before the bowel becomes completely clean.

In my case, I have "been to the river" over 1000 times, or I have had over 1000 "reed treatments" during this time I have learned many extraordinary things about the bowel of which I became absolutely certain. After witnessing old feces that were putrefied and fermented for several years, the water ran clean. After that, it is clear that the food is in transit for approximately 13 to 15 hours, from mouth to anus. When you reach this place, it is very clear what is what, and of course your amazing energy levels will be the true witness. Muscle testing to ask the body how many colonics it needs is very erroneous. God has already established the protocol in the Dead Sea Scrolls and that is to clean your bowel until the "water runs clear".

CHAPTER 17

The Big Awakening

Remember this truth—there is a huge difference between partial and sporadic application and the complete practice of a principle. This holds true when spirituality is applied towards any of the four bodies: physical, mental, emotion, and spiritual.

For example, you could attend church once a week and feel the spirit as you pray, sing praises, gaze upon your fellow brothers and sisters with loving eyes, feeling overwhelmed with the wonderful love of God in your heart. For the rest of the week, you may deny a brother or sister in need of forgiveness (or whatever their need), glare at a co-worker, and basically shut off the spirit of God from flowing abundantly through you each waking moment.

Similarly, I have seen fear and misunderstanding when it comes to cleansing the physical body, even amongst professionals practicing colon hygiene. The question is, how colonics is used as a tool—advising of the once-in-a-while colonic verses the consecutive colonic. I have found that fear gets promoted by those who have not submitted themselves to the truth by allowing their own body to teach them the truth. Fear never takes you where you want to go. Practicing colon hygiene religiously (once in a while) may appear as if you are health conscious. But the practice of colonics spiritually, would mean releasing all the old feces out systematically until the water runs clear. It is simply the difference between religion and spirituality! There is a BIG difference, one works, one doesn't.

On the other hand, experts in colon hygiene have proven it to work successfully by their own vibrant and healthy life. Dr. Bernard Jensen and Dr. Norman Walker are two of the greatest examples of the consecutive colonic to clear out back-up waste. If you have never seen a photo of either of these two men, you should! You will not find anybody healthier than the people who choose to use colon hygiene in accordance with the Dead Sea Scrolls.

Bernard Jensen discovered this the hard way. As a doctor of Naturopathy, he did all the right things using herbs, nutrition, and exercise, and he STILL got cancer. So he aggressively cleaned his bowel and became cancer-free once he removed the toxic waste from his body.

Any fear that you might harm your bowel from doing too many colonics is erroneous! The bowel is something like a memory bank. It has been stuffed so full for so long that for most people, it has shut down. We have trained it to only work when overfilled to capacity. So it becomes lazy. Even if you switched your diet to all raw food, the peristalsis has gone dormant and the bowel will continue to fill to overcapacity before it will release. It requires serious reprogramming.

Having a colonic once a week or once a month clears space in the rectum temporarily. Most likely, you will not have a bowel movement the next day because it is trained to remain stuck. The feces simply move down to fill the space to overcapacity again. The bowel must be shifted from stuck-mode to the function for which it was designed.

There is abundant work to be done! As a culture we must change our programming from "fallen" toward fullness with truth. This only is accomplished by alignment with truth, a truth we cannot even comprehend because of the filth held in our bodies. The moment of change begins when we ask to be taught. Meekness comes first. Meanwhile, the ego will tell us that we are fine the way we are. Once you start doing systematic colonics, you will laugh at this denial.

When you choose to utilize colon hygiene, as directed in the Dead Sea Scrolls until the water runs clean, you open the way for positive change. In fact, you have subjected your ego to your higher self and now the programming of "holding on" changes to "letting go." The body aligns with truth and opens up, contrary to fear-based suppression in our culture that has led to this great shutting down.

If you think about it, every wonderful healing modality process works by letting go, whether emotional, structural, or biochemical. So it is especially true for the bowel. Look around and you will see that this country is in a serious health crisis (and emotional crisis!). Do not change if that is what you want to be a part of.

Colonics are actually hilarious. Once you make the decision to cleanse your body, your higher self is giddy with the result—the release of all the wonderful stuck putrification and fermentation that we fought so long to hold onto because of our fear! Your face and eyes start to sparkle, old aches and pains one-by-one may disappear, and best of all, you experience renewed high energy levels. All your life your body has been begging for an internal bath and you did not even know it! When you get to this place you reach the blessedness of knowing what it means to truly love yourself. Colonics open the way for this great awakening.

No other healing modality is spoken of in the Bible that by doing it, "your eyes will see" and "your ears will hear." This takes us into the spiritual realm.

The physical body has an important role in spirituality and is the "activator" to the mind, emotions, and spirit. Even if a specific health issue is not based in the physical body, cleansing it helps tremendously to trigger the release of underlying causes. By responding to the truth of cleansing, the full blessings and rewards come.

In the previous decades and centuries, the Earth was cleaner. Now we have more work to do on the physical plane just to get clean enough to activate basic energy work. And in order for us to awaken and ascend, energy is necessary.

CHAPTER 18

It's the Real Booty Call

How was it that in biblical times people lived almost 1000 years? How did they harness that energy that enabled their long lives? It appears that we have traded long life in for a short life of abuse. If we are to tap into true vitality and health, we must return to the ancient mysteries and practices that bring longevity.

In my opinion, the time is NOW. This new century is an age of information, yet that information has come full circle. The keys and codes of the ancients are simply returning to us so that our lives can be enriched for our spiritual advancement. The Dead Sea Scrolls state: "All manner of disease is removed through the bowel." Let's not miss it this time! Advanced colon hygiene is absolutely necessary in this day and time to remove toxicity. The ancient healing practices have erroneously been replaced and now we can see our collective health is worse than ever.

Clean bodies are critical to the spirit. In order for the "higher self" to actualize, it must integrate the person physically, emotionally, and mentally. This comes through the heart and not the intellect (conforming not to this world) and by recognizing and following certain universal laws.

The spirit cannot habitat in a toxic or "low vibration" body. The weakest aspects of the full body are the emotional and mental bodies. By the law of attraction, a clean body draws to itself a higher vibration in the mind and emotions. Simply by cleansing the body, the vibration level of the person rises and thus enables the higher self to integrate a greater sense of oneness with the self, others, and God.

Ridding ourselves of blockages helps us achieve union with our Heavenly Father through the Light. Our goal should be to use our energy wisely to reach toward higher vibration levels of Light and peace. Ironically, as the mental and emotional garbage is shed, the body bears the weight of this toxic release. That is why this is a process of an upward spiral and colonics can be a basal key to start the flow and keep it going.

We have all heard that we are to be good stewards of "our Temples." Now you know why. It may not be easy to forsake the negative ego, but as the Holy Spirit teaches, you soon discover that the truth is simple. Move forward in love and light, my brothers and sisters. This is the BIG AWAKENING!

CHAPTER 19

The News of the Weird

This interesting article appeared in the News of the Weird, The Nashville Scene, May 31, 2001.

A Vancouver, British Columbia, apartment complex was evacuated and condemned in April after a dentist died inhaling toxic vapors while engaging in his at-home hobby of fooling around with his large collection of mercury. And in Cardington, Ohio, after chemist Thomas Beiter died of apparently natural causes in his apartment in February, authorities found 17 pounds of mercury and two containers of uranium, with which, according to his brother, he liked to conduct various experiments in his home laboratory.

My reaction…and we are told that heavy metals in our dental work are safe!

CHAPTER 20

January 2001

It is now January 2001. I will fill you in on the year between April 2000, when my first book was completely written and January 2001, when my first book became available to the public.

In April 2000, my physical body was in a release mode that was initiated in June of 1999 and is still continuing. If you remember, my body was detoxing heavy metals as a result of mercury dental filling removal. Also remember, my body was a clean slate when it came to other health care issues. It has taken one year and six months for my body to get to a certain level of environmental cleanliness—free of the poisoning that is the result of dental chemicals. Remember also, that I was moving aggressively with an already clean body.

The outward manifestation of this poison removal is very obvious. Although people do not totally understand this process, many people in my community have stopped me with many questions. Even though I had dropped forty pounds, it is obvious that my body has regenerated to a point of vitality that could never have come from synthetics or just weight loss. There is no placebo affect when it comes to real vitality and health. When the proper things are done, the results are real and lasting. Now you can continue in these steps to insure your good health for the rest of your life.

I want the public to know that this did not have to cost an arm and a leg, just dedication to the truth and application of this information! I only used Natural Vegetable Glycerin, the NOW brand and KANTITA, from Kroeger Herb Inc. for yeast removal. Also, it is important to understand that the poison has to come out of the body cavity completely and systematically with colonics. This step CANNOT be left out!

This procedure does not have to be an expensive endeavor. There are Colema Boards you can purchase for very small amounts of money and you can have a colonic unit installed in your home. No one can ever stop you from getting healed in the privacy of your own home. Remember God gave YOU this responsibility, so he designed our bodies in the manner he did so that we could have the tools and means to accomplish this task and responsibility within our daily routines. Remember God tells us in the DEAD SEA SCROLLS why and how to go down to the river and clean your bowel. The river was public domain. I am sure the river water contained microorganisms!

It would be giving your power and your ability to evolve away if you allowed another human being to be in charge of your health care! Others may help, but you are in the driver's seat. You cannot use the excuse that you cannot afford it.

Also, I must make this statement because it is the truth. I have never had one chelation treatment. My point is that it does not have to cost anybody a lot of money to become truly well. If you learn to understand herbs, supplements, and foods, you will understand how to use these effectively. I have seen in the last two years a lot of new products that work to remove heavy metals from the body. Unfortunately, the American people cannot afford to get well even in the holistic community because of greed. Just as they cannot afford to be kept ill by the alternative of traditional ill health care! It is my belief that if a health care professional is making their living predominately by the sale of and the over-charging of supplements, that they have not developed their individual or unique gift ministry or healing art. So I exhort you to get on with your own healing process, practitioner, so that you can do the unique things for others that a supplement company cannot do for them.

CHAPTER 21

The Philosophy of One Century is the Common Sense of the Next

The philosophy of one century is the common sense of the next. This incredible truth comes from a fortune cookie that I received after dinner in my favorite Chinese restaurant! The wonderful thing about truth is that it has existed since the beginning of time and we just get to rediscover it as we live our lifetimes. There is really "nothing new under the sun" and there is no point in "reinventing the wheel." But obviously and relentlessly man's ego continues to try. Unfortunately, the cost is many innocent lives, always!

Think about prohibition and the price that was paid in innocent lives just because of the legality of alcohol. It was a battle over who would control the profits, rather than about the safety of the people. And now we can sit at a bar or restaurant and have a beer without it costing many lives.

As I studied the Reformation and Martin Luther, I was amazed how many lives were destroyed before and as a result of this man's discovery of truth that was right there in front of everyone's nose all along. Right in the Holy Scriptures, that of course everyone must have read from time to time.

At this time, the Holy Roman Catholic Church was charging money to be paid by the people (sinners) in order to remove an individual's sin! Funk and Wagnall's standard college dictionary says concerning this practice of indulgences: "In the Roman Catholic Church, remission of temporal punishment due for a sin after it has been forgiven through sacramental absolution." It's interesting how the individual's money played a part in the sacramental absolution! Luther rediscovered in the scriptures that "hey, we do not need to buy our way out of sin." The Holy Scriptures say that we are saved by grace! "For grace are ye saved through faith; and that not of yourselves; it is the gift of God." (Ephesians 2:8).

They were living in the administration of grace that God had ordained after our Lord and Savior gave his life for our forgiveness of sins. So why were men still paying other men for their sins? Jesus Christ was "now" the only mediation between man and God, not any church or man's doctrine. The New Testament is full of liberation from sin and bondage through grace. How was this tragedy occurring when the truth was right there in front of them in the scriptures? Men changing the truth into the form of a lie just to serve their own egos, all under the disguise of "RELIGION".

When Luther started preaching and teaching the truth, he had to hide for many years because the wonderful religious leaders wanted to kill him. Why? Because he screwed up their racketeering! If you have never educated yourself concerning this time period, you really should. It shows how ignorance of the truth will always put us in a devastating and vulnerable state in our lives, and that others will most certainly use our ignorance against us. Remember God tells us in I Timothy 2:4, "Who will have all men to be saved, and to come unto the knowledge of truth." Remember, God says that his people are destroyed for a lack of knowledge!

This time period was a great example of these truths. Now in this day and time, "everybody knows" that "we are saved by grace." It is a simple truth that we almost take for granted as common sense today.

Perhaps the common sense of bowel cleansing during biblical days will become more than just philosophy of this century and hopefully thousands of lives will not have to be sacrificed because of man's ego! In addition to bowel cleansing there were other common sense tools utilized during biblical years that are recorded in the historical scriptures. These modalities brought great healing to the people of that day and time. They still work and are available during this century, if we have the common sense to utilize them.

CHAPTER 22

The Jabez Prayer

If one has not received the blessing, which comes from reading the book, "The Prayer Of Jabez", you can. I feel inspired to bless this book with this wonderfully inspirational information based in truth. I am certain you will be blessed by it.

"And Jabez called on the God of Israel saying, "Oh, that You would bless me indeed, and enlarge my territory, that Your hand would be with me, and that You would keep me from evil, that I may not cause pain!" So God granted him what he requested."

If any human being makes this request to God, they will be granted this. Just understand as Jabez did, that there would be plenty of work and accountability involved, followed by much healing and joy.

The name Jabez means, "pain". The literal rendering in Hebrew could read, "He causes (or will cause) pain." I believe this story is chosen to be revealed biblically and historically because it is applicable to every human being. In order for any of us to leave the level of existence we are at and to further grow in love and light, which will only play out in greater service to God, in a larger territory, it will be a painful but fulfilling venture. As Jabez accomplished this, he allowed the Holy Spirit to work through him so that the greatness of God would be manifested by him. It did require Jabez's free will decision of obedience to do the plan. God blessed Jabez, and Jabez received the blessings. He allowed his life to be used within the Divine Plan. He allowed the truth to dictate his pace. Why not pray this simple but powerful prayer for your life?

CHAPTER 23

A Heavy Metals News Flash

It is with MUCH humbleness of self and with great illumination that I offer up this information from both experience and from SPIRIT in this chapter of this second book to you.

I decided many years ago to submit my ego to my HIGHER SELF and as these scriptures expand on this endeavor in Romans 12:1: "I beseech you therefore, brethren, by the mercies of God, that ye present your bodies a living sacrifice, holy, acceptable unto God, which is your reasonable (logical) service."

Verse 2: "And BE NOT CONFORMED TO THIS WORLD: but be ye transformed by the renewing of your mind, that ye may prove what is that good, and acceptable, and perfect will of God."

Verse 3: "For I say, through the grace given unto me, to EVERY man that is among you, NOT TO THINK OF HIMSELF MORE HIGHLY THAN HE OUGHT TO THINK (man's ego); but to think soberly, according as God hath dealt to every man the measure of faith." (Each man subjecting himself, by choice, to his higher self, which is in total alignment with the scriptures and God's will.)

This is the standard for all of us. As each individual decides to subject themselves to the truth, their life will change drastically and wonderfully. The work is laborious though, and this is where the confusion comes in. This is the work that we are to do in our lifetimes. What our paradigms are and what the truth is are definitely two different things! As we release our egos (and corresponding paradigms) we change our thought process of error to the truth, which is what our higher self will then teach us since our HIGHER SELF IS CONNECTED TO THE GODHEAD!

But God will never violate your free will, which is why you must consciously and by deliberate decision subject yourself to the information and then the carrying out of that information in order to obtain the full reward or benefit. This takes researching the scriptures, understanding that the GIFT MINISTRIES are here for this work. Taking the time and money to complete these tasks, and the culmination will be the life situations that will then arise to challenge you to carry out the new truth that you have learned.

Ultimately all these tasks rest on your shoulders, not anybody else's, not your spouse, not your parent, not your employer, not your brother, nor your sister, not your clergyman, not your government, not your doctor, not your health care provider nor your insurance company. Your HIGHER SELF will direct you to the individuals who will lovingly educate you in order to help you find the truth and then carry it out. They will NEVER intimidate you, NEVER come from a fear-based motive, and NEVER violate your free will! If your free will is EVER violated and you are ever forced to do anything against your will, legally or illegally, that situation is NEVER in alignment with your HIGHER SELF or THE GODHEAD!

We are living in times that the only thing that will save us is our obedience to the truth. Whether the so-called "experts" are acknowledging that we are polluted with high levels of heavy metals or not. The manifestations of disastrous health issues are quickly escalating in this country. The WALL STREET JOURNAL published an article in March 2001 stating that the government had tested a select group of Americans for heavy metals. All those tested contained high levels of heavy metals in their bodies. At the conclusion, it stated that there was still NO connection with disease and heavy metals. What do you think?

1) Never in the history of mankind has this level of pollution and so many heavy metals been in our environment. That is why the medical community is having such a hard time figuring this out; these are new environmental illness born from ignorance and greed. We do not have textbook bodies, but we do have extremely polluted bodies that cannot take one more synthetic anything, least of all more drugs!

This is another reason why most EVERYBODY is experiencing allergies to everything under the sun. It is not the organic products causing intolerance, but the maxed out polluted bodies (bowels and livers) that cannot tolerate one more thing. And of course, as soon as you begin to cleanse the bowel, relief is immediate.

2) The second scenario manifesting is this: people are removing their metal fillings and replacing them with who knows what! First, you can utilize a bio-energy machine to match the proper compatible materials for your mouth. Next, the people that have their metal fillings removed and do absolutely nothing to chelate the metals through their systems and out of the body cavity with systematic colonics will manifest many horrible health conditions. Now remember, this was the condition that manifested in me for two years beginning in 1997. I was not chelating the heavy metals through my body cavity, but was doing colonics. You will gain about 25 pounds or lose considerable weight because the metals interfere with vitamin and mineral absorption in the small intestine (celiac disease). I blew up like a "dough girl" within those two years.

I experienced panic attacks consistently—my head felt like it was going to blow off my neck. (Which sounds like symptoms of a stroke.) Remember from my first book, when I realized this and implemented the chelation process. I utilized Natural Vegetable Glycerin and Kantita to pull the heavy metals and yeast from all parts of my body cavity and into my bowel. Immediately the panic attacks stopped, my head no longer felt any pressure and I dropped the excess weight. Our health issues go far beyond diet and exercise in these days.

It is imperative when dental work is done and the metals are removed, to immediately start pulling the metals through with a chelating substance. If you fail to do this, the metals will deposit throughout the body, causing many health issues. Once the metals are released into the blood stream, keep them moving out, for a quick exit out the bowel using systematic colonics.

3) So this brings us to the third scenario. There will be people who remove the metals from dental work and chelate, but who will not do colonics, or will not do enough colonics to accommodate the chelation process and these people will become very, very, very septic. The kidneys may go into failure because there will not be an equaled release accommodation between the kidneys and bowel, unless colonics are utilized at this specific juncture. Without the systematic colonics the kidneys cannot handle the volume and intensity of these metals and may fail. I fell into this category and became the first case study to learn this from and then to address it successfully. This truth surpasses the traditional medical community's understanding of the causes and dangers of heavy metal toxicity. First, a person must clean up their organs and systems by ridding the body of putrid waste and parasites. As the body begins to detox, you can begin stepping up the cleansing process, as many as 3 to 5 colonics per week will provide the necessary release of toxins. If you slack on this point, you will become even more ill. I know this from a lot of experience. If you have your dental work replaced, even by the best dentist, and you chelate using the best products and methods, but fail to do 3 to 5 colonics per week in order to pull the heavy metals and old fecal waste out completely, your system will become very septic. This condition manifests with severe headaches,

constant sore throats and glands, pain throughout the tissues, muscles and organs, insomnia, and feeling so lethargic you will not want to get out of bed. Interestingly, these symptoms sound very similar to symptoms of the major diseases we are witnessing. They also sound like the symptoms listed on the drug advertisements on the television.

PEOPLE—please understand that the ego has convinced us that we are well. Also, there is always room for improvement. If we were really well in this country, why is disease so rampant? Why do people get treated for diseases and never fully recover but just manage them? What are all the birth defects caused by and why are young people so sick and dying so young? When you view film footage from any time before and including the 1960's, people are vibrant and 99% of them are lean. Presently people all ages are over weight and toxic looking all the way around. Do you really think the little fishes in the sea are so full of mercury that they are the cause of this heavy metal pollution we are bearing? But the vast volume of heavy metals put into our mouths every year really could not be the cause of any of this disease that we are witnessing and experiencing. What do you think? If I heard Wilt Chamberlain's daughter correctly during the press conference addressing his passing several years ago, she said that her father had been in excellent health and that he had just had extensive dental work done previous to his passing. She appeared to be in shock.

Consider also that people are on all sorts of anti-depressants. Children are put on Ritalin just because they may be a bit to toxic and cannot concentrate. So our culture being as it is, pushes to hide those pollution problems with more pollution. We have replaced our hygienic practices of old with new poisons. Are we willing to sacrifice the health of our own children in order to appear intelligent and mainstream? Have we given our power away? Or are we willing to allow our hearts to lead us in seeking truth in order to gain the insight on exactly what these children may need? Do you really know all the ingredients in the immunizations that are given to our children? Are you really educated on these matters or do you proceed blindly because you think that everything that is legal has to be good for you?

I know personally of young people suffering with strokes and heart attacks after having dental work done. I have witnessed women miscarrying directly after having dental work done. People are living with frequent panic attacks, as I personally did after dental procedures for a three-year period. They stopped completely after several years of heavy metal environmental clean-up.

PEOPLE if we were WELL for real, we would be manifesting and witnessing wellness! There is no placebo for true vitality and health.

CHAPTER 24

Process of Discovering Real Personal Wellness

Now, I will share the last bit of information from SPIRIT. I will quickly recap from my first book the process of discovering real personal wellness and the healing of my entire "temple" from 1987 through 1996. I cleaned my bowel entirely with frequent colonics, purged my organs of all types of bacteria and parasites, and then rebuilt my organs and systems with organic foods and food complexes. Then as you may recall, I conducted much research on the connection between heavy metal poisoning from dental work and all manner of disease. At that time there was very little information about how to remove heavy metals from the body cavity. I still proceeded in this direction regardless.

Here is what I learned: The dental fillings in the mouth are not fit for the human body. These heavy metals consist of mercury, silver, aluminum, and many other metals that are documented in many books available today. This information is based on verifiable facts. I have compiled a list at the beginning of this book for referencing.

These various metals will leak slowly during years of wear and tear; eating, brushing, dental cleaning, etc. As these metals are released, they lodge throughout various parts of the human body. The favorite accumulations seem to be in the reproductive organs, both in the male and female. They manifest in all the various cancers that we are seeing. Also, the metals will cause the immune system to not work optimally so that parasite activity becomes out of control, specifically in the joints and muscles. These manifest as other diseases such as fibromyalgia, lupus, multiple sclerosis, etc.

These poisons will flow throughout your formally organic body. Your brain becomes foggy, and you will literally feel insane. Your nervous system will become a total mess. How do I know this? Because I personally experienced every one of these symptoms following the removal of my dental fillings during 1996 and 1997. I have also witnessed these symptoms with many other people during the last several years. The bottom lying cause will always trigger many other symptoms that also need to be addressed. These symptoms seem to disappear eventually as the predominate cause is removed. When the heavy metals leave the body cavity (you can see them through the tube), when enough of them have exited, then the other symptoms seem to disappear.

    I am writing this last segment of this book on April 14, 2001. Which is approximately 4 years after the removal of those heavy metal fillings, along with 4 years of various cleansing strategies. I removed my fillings, cleaned my bowel without chelating, and finally after chelating this is what happened. This unfortunately has happened to thousands of people now and will in the future. I have just experienced a serious health crisis that thankfully brought "my temple" to a much higher plane of exuberant living! You see by 1999 I realized that I needed to chelate the metals through many physical levels and systems using vegetable glycerin. However, I had reduced my colonics to twice per month. (Remember from my charts the many colonics I had done over 10 years) A person might wonder after so many, how could a human being still need to do more? Well the lesson from the universe is still the same: LET THE RESULTS DICTATE THE PACE! As I was starting to chelate the heavy metals from my system, I was not accommodating my body for the final release of poison to exit from kidney to bowel then bowel to anus for the final exit. This could have been accomplished all along had I been doing a colonic per day or even one every other day. This meant that the metals were being stored in my kidneys throughout these four years. I will always be in "AWE" at the body's ability to protect itself! It has always amazed me how close to death's door one can come just from pollution, even if the body is basically healthy otherwise. Now, almost four years of pioneering through the heavy metal removal, my body was going into "septic shock" or most likely may have been labeled medically as "kidney failure". I did not go to the hospital because of this: If the medical community is not honestly researching this subject, then they would not treat it accurately and therefore putting my life in even greater risk. I perceived that they would try to counter act the activity in my kidneys with yet another poisonous drug, which would easily cause my death. I was not willing to take that chance. It was obvious that poison was throwing my body into shock. Because of the very close monitoring of my body for so many years, I was absolutely sure, the only thing that could be causing this problem would have to be the heavy metals accumulating in the kidneys. I knew from previous experience and research that I was in the best possible hands that I could be in, God's and my own! I decided to step up the release of these metals by doing a colonic every day. During this release, I saw the reddish brown sludge that I had witnessed in other similar cases. The odor is that of a very "skunky" origin. This is the type of material that collects in the kidneys when they are overwhelmed with metal they cannot release normally. (Because we were NEVER meant to have these in our system) In my fifteen years of research, I have only witnessed this process when dealing with people who have fully committed to dental removal from the mouth. These people follow up with the complete chelating of heavy metals from their system and organs, followed by the culmination of removal of poisons from kidney, to bowel, to exit out of the body completely, which of course, means systematic colonics. There are many people that have witnessed this process and are very familiar with the appearance and odor of these insidious heavy metals.

When I was in this state of shock, I was shaking violently. I had really never been in such pain with the exception of childbirth, but at least then I could get some relief with the process of the birth. The relief would only come with the exiting of the heavy metals. The three tank colonics that I was doing was not accommodating the full release that I needed. This was because the three tank or twenty minute colonic brought the metals from the kidneys into the cecum and would shoot the metals back into the bloodstream throwing me back into shock. The spirit told me to stay up on the table until I saw the reddish brown sludge come through the tube. This ended up being a five tank or forty minute colonic. I have never required this type of colonic before because my bowel was totally clean, but for this particular situation it was the necessary utilization of this tool in order to complete the task at hand. Therefore, it did not send the metals back through the cecum into my bloodstream again, but by- passed the cecum and continued to pull the metals from the cecum area through to the anus and down the drain. My body was so relieved.

I did go into shock several more times during this week. The reason was this, I should have done a colonic twice a day so the metals would not have gotten to recirculate through my cecum at the intervals that they did. I should have stepped up the removal process. I learned this with hindsight, but as I kept moving at the slower pace eventually each day, with each colonic, I witnessed less and less reddish brown sludge and odor. So, then I backed down to one colonic every other day, until I saw very little sludge. Then I backed down to every two days, then every three days then every four days, then five days. Today I have two to three bowel movements per day and every five days I have a three tank colonic that is moderate. I keep my body clean to that level.

My choice of maintenance of INTERNAL HYGIENE is this pace because my energy levels do not fluctuate and my diet stays moderate. The results dictate the pace. I do what it takes to stay at this level of health and vitality, much like my exercise program, message program, business program, marriage program, etc. You get the idea!

Natural Vegetable Glycerin is a very good chelator. It is an ingredient used in kidney cleansing. The symptoms that I had during chelation were extremely intense. I experienced aching pain from my head to my toes. I could literally feel every organ on fire. My reproductive organs were very sore. Muscle testing kept saying that I was in premature menopause. I am convinced that the wear on the reproductive organs is so great from the heavy metals, that this is the cause of problems for many women that are experiencing so call premature menopausal issues. We need to come even further out of the "nine dots" so to speak. Broaden our understanding these days. These heavy metals change all the dynamics of health care diagnosis.

My back near my kidneys was soooooo painful, and my colon felt sore and full of bacteria. My immune system had been running so low for the past two years, because of the heavy metals, that I had picked up more bacterial and viral infections during these two years than ever in all my life. The first day that I went into shock I consulted with a colleague in order to support myself comfortably until the removal was completed. My body tested for 800 mg of ibuprofen every 4 hours to help keep me from going into shock, but I actually used it in order to bring me out of shock. I was sweating and freezing simultaneously. In my solar plexus area I felt intense pain and sweating with heat flashes. It was the only pain that I ever experienced that was greater than childbearing. I shook violently and my face turned snow white and my lips became very purple. I estimate that I went into shock over seven times in seven days. There were three witnesses throughout these seven days. As the ibuprofen would begin to work I would meditate and do yoga breathing to pull myself through it. Of course, I realized nothing would pull the poison out except colonics, so I was in the best possible place. My body muscle tested for eight red raspberry two times per day for five days. These supported my reproductive organs. I believe the heavy metals are utilized as the physical root cause for most of the female reproductive issues. I believe premature menopausal issues are included in this.

I believe that the question format involved with muscle testing techniques needs to be updated and integrated with advanced colon cleansing technique information in order to get more accurate information during crisis situations. The accuracy of the information coming through with muscle testing is only as accurate as the questions that are fed into the innate. The resource of information needs to become broader and updated. We need to work together better as professionals and healers.

I also tested for bacteria and Streptococcus. This was handled by a homeopathic tincture from Hanna Kroeger electro magnetically attuned to a specific frequency 6x potency. The Strep will lie dormant for years in the deep cavities of the body, especially in connection with the cavitations in the mouth and extracted tooth areas. It will surface when the stress levels of the body escalate during these types of situations. I also felt that my body needed help kicking the bacteria out, and understood that the presence of the heavy metals would make that a difficult task. My body's intelligence utilized this formula as a natural antibiotic as it muscle tested for forty drops of Echinacea every two hours for five cycles. The other herb that helped was Pau d'Arco bark, twenty-six drops every two hours for four cycles. By the end of the day, my body shifted to a safer place and I continued the integration of all these excellent tools.

With the systematic implementations of the correct tools, my health improved immediately. After one solid month, all the heavy metals were completely out of my body. The level of health that I escalated into was phenomenal! The peacefulness was graciously accepted. My sleep during the night became extremely peaceful, restful, and healing. Just as a baby's. My outward appearance changed immensely. The people that saw me on a daily basis commented! I am thankful to be on the labor-intensive side of work needed for an individual to come full circle with health. You will need to find a dentist that understands this subject matter and is open to doing better dental care. You will need compatibility testing. Compatibility testing will ensure that the dental materials are compatible with your blood and body type. A bio-energy machine can do this. Also, during the dental work, this machine will test the cavitation to ensure complete bacterial removal. Then last and MOST IMPORTANTLY remove all the heavy metals out through your bowel or all these poisons WILL recirculate through your body causing even more harm than before!

Let me please speak some illuminating words of comfort to you. The reason that this healing process was sometimes difficult for me is because there was close to no information out there concerning this. Next, I have not met another human being that has gone this far with the removal process. I have met some people that have done pieces of this process, but that is all. Therefore, I feel that I was very much on my own. I also understand that it is the pioneering individual that has the responsibility and privilege to bring this truth into a world that is motivated by greed and in agreement to conceal truth. I gave my permission to the universe, to utilize me, in order to help bring the truth in. I felt completely protected the whole decade I researched and dedicated my live body to this. Now we know how to bring people through more comfortably, and of course, more safely. I ask that anyone who reads this book that is in any health situation to demand to be tested for heavy metals. It is my opinion that you will find that the heavy metals in your body cavity will play a major part in any health crisis.

Hopefully, the systematic process of colonic irrigation will be incorporated into our health care systems because of our continued educational pursuits. All these wonderful things that we can do for ourselves will only bring us to a better place in all of our bodies, emotionally, mentally, physically and spiritually. We can back the linear timeline up and actually go across time into REGENERATION!

CHAPTER 25

Advance Colon Hygiene May Lead To Regeneration

Remember colonics may be used in many situations and in many ways. First, you may wish to clean your total bowel to bring your body to its purest state. I like to call it a clean slate. Of course, you know from this research, that it may take many years depending on your commitment and schedule. Remember, it will take approximately 15 colonics x your age = total colonics. You divide that into 365 days of the year and set the pace to your comfort zone. 7 days a week is safe. Remember when there is nothing left in your bowel you will be able to clearly tell through the tube.

Second, colonics may be utilized when you have a fever. Several times over the last decade when I picked up bacteria, a virus, or ran a fever, it was a quick colonic that pulled it right out of my body almost immediately. The quicker the germ leaves the body, the faster the body recovers.

Third, if you get food poisoning at any time, a quick colonic may bring this bacteria right out of the body, which will bring you quickly back into balance. Remember though, if the body is in the process of cleansing over the years, the quick colonics may just move the poison to another place in your bowel temporarily. This is because the bowel is still very full and will not function as optimally as it will once the total cleaning is complete.

Fourth, the hydration process that occurs from the colonics can be very healing at any time for whatever reason you may have become dehydrated. Constipation and a full bowel cause dehydration. The water in the body is always being stolen from various other places and jobs in order to aid the constant state of survival mode in the bowel department. Cleaning your bowel requires a large amount of water because the old hardened feces have to be remoisturized in order to soften. When you have made the decision to clean the bowel the body will change the programming over from storage to release. The old hardened feces have to change consistency in order to create movement to move through the bowel. Although fifteen gallons of water are utilized during the procedure, not all of this water goes into the bowel directly, but is used in the process of the system of the unit. Approximately two quarts of water are utilized within the bowel itself. People see immediate change in their skin texture and color because colonics are so hydrating.

Fifth, colonics may be very helpful in showing other organ dysfunction. As the bowel cleanses it takes tremendous pressure off the other organs. The other organs begin to detox and release, displaying symptoms in other parts of the body. This is very good. Keep cleansing and rebuilding those organs. As the bacteria leaves through the cleansing, the organs will regenerate and heal. Healing and regeneration will occur when the toxins are completely removed and the rebuilding is completed with the introduction of the eight strands of intestinal flora and a complete source of minerals. Glandulars will also aid in the rebuilding process especially with each individual organ. You may rebuild your organs with bovine organ (glandulars). The flora and minerals need to be ingested after each colonic so the body has a twenty-four hour period to completely utilize these substances in order to receive the full benefit of each. When the internal organs are functioning optimally, you will witness the change outwardly. Advanced colon hygiene can only lead to regeneration.

Documentation of Bowel Management: 1987-1992

1987 – 1988 – 1989 – 1990 – 1991 – 1992

7 Day Colon Cleanse

Psyllium Seed	Bentonnite	Distilled Water	No Food	Green Magma	1 coffee Enema
4x per day	4x per day	All Day		6 tablets, 4x per day	Per day

Followed this procedure every six months from **1987** to July of **1992**. From August 1992 thru October 1993 – approximately 100 colonics until colon was completely clean. The water ran clear; no black, old feces ever came thru the tube again.

Apr. 1993	May 1993	June 1993	July 1993	Aug. 1993	Sept 1993	Oct. 1993	Nov. 1993	Dec. 1993
4/21	5/1	6/3	7/4	8/6	9/1	10/5	11/3	12/1
4/23	5/4	6/15	7/15	8/11	9/3	10/24	11/10	12/11
	5/7		7/16	8/15	9/8	*Colon Clean	11/15	12/12
	5/10		7/25	8/16	9/10		11/19	12/17
	5/14		7/27	8/17	9/23		11/29	12/22
	5/17			8/18	9/27			12/23
	5/20			8/20	9/28			12/24
	5/22							12/25
	5/24							
	5/27							

Jan. 1994	Feb. 1994	March 1994	April 1994	May 1994	June 1994
1/6	2/1	3/1	4/1	5/4	6/5
1/7	2/3	3/3	4/5	5/5	6/7
1/8	2/9	3/4	4/11	5/11	6/8
1/10	2/14	3/10	4/19	5/12	6/9
1/12	2/19	3/11	4/21	5/14	6/10
1/13	2/25	3/18	4/22	5/20	6/17

1/15		3/23	4/23	5/25	6/21
1/17		3/27	4/24	5/31	6/25
1/20			4/25		6/27
1/27			4/26		
1/29			4/28		

July 1994	Aug. 1994	Sept. 1994	Oct. 1994	Nov. 1994	Dec. 1994
7/3	8/1	9/2	10/2	11/1	12/4
7/7	8/2	9/3	10/3	11/2	12/6
7/11	8/3	9/4	10/4	11/3	12/8
7/12	8/4	9/5	10/5	11/4	12/10
7/13	8/5	9/6	10/6	11/5	12/12
7/14	8/6	9/7	10/7	11/6	12/14
7/15	8/7	9/8	10/8	11/7	12/15
7/17	8/8	9/11	10/9	11/8	12/16
7/20	8/9	9/12	10/10	11/9	12/18
7/21	8/10	9/13	10/11	11/10	12/19
7/23	8/11	9/14	10/12	11/12	12/22
7/24	8/12	9/21	10/13	11/13	12/23
7/25	8/13	9/23	10/14	11/17	12/25
7/26	8/14	9/24	10/15	11/18	12/28
7/27	8/15	9/26	10/16	11/21	12/30
7/28	8/16	9/27	10/18	11/22	12/31
7/29	8/17	9/28	10/19	11/24	
7/30	8/1	9/29	10/20	11/27	
7/31	8/21	9/30	10/23	11/29	
	8/22		10/24		
	8/23		10/25		
	8/25		10/26		
	8/26		10/27		
	8/27		10/28		
	8/28		10/29		
	8/29		10/30		
	8/31		10/31		

Jan. 1995	Feb. 1995	March 1995	April 1995	May 1995	June 1995
1/2	2/2	3/10	4/1	5/20	6/4
1/6	2/4	3/16	4/7	5/24	6/6
1/7	2/5	3/20	4/9	5/28	6/12
1/9	2/6	3/21	4/17		6/24

1/10	2/6	3/25	4/21		
1/11	2/8		4/22		
1/12	2/12		4/23		
1/13	2/13		4/26		
1/14			4/29		
1/15					
1/16					
1/18					
1/19					
1/23					
1/24					
1/25					
1/26					
1/27					

July 1995	Aug. 1995	Sept. 1995	Oct. 1995	Nov. 1995	Dec. 1995
7/9	8/7	9/6	10/3	11/2	12/11
7/16	8/16	9/15	10/6	11/10	12/19
7/25	8/22	9/20	10/11	11/17	12/27
7/29	8/28	9/22	10/17	11/23	
		9/23	10/26		

Jan. 1996	Feb. 1996	March 1996	April 1996	May 1996	June 1996
1/6	2/2	3/7		5/16	6/10
1/11	2/10	3/16		5/25	6/21
1/21	2/16	3/27			
1/26	2/23				

July 1996	Aug. 1996	Sept. 1996	Oct. 1996	Nov. 1996	Dec. 1996
7/22	8/29	9/4	10/4	11/4	12/26
			10/28	11/30	

Jan. 1997	Feb. 1997	March 1997	April 1997	May 1997	June 1997
1/19	2/9	3/3	4/3	5/2	6/4
		3/15	4/5	5/5	6/8
		3/21	4/8	5/8	6/11
		3/25	4/12	5/11	6/15
		3/28	4/16	5/14	6/19

		3/31	4/19	5/17	6/22
			4/23	5/18	6/25
			4/25	5/25	6/29
			4/28	5/28	
				5/31	

July 1997	Aug. 1997	Sept. 1997	Oct. 1997	Nov. 1997	Dec. 1997
7/4	8/1	9/1	10/1	11/1	12/8
7/7	8/5	9/4	10/3	11/8	12/14
7/10	8/8	9/7	10/6	11/17	12/22
7/15	8/11	9/14	10/10	11/28	12/30
7/18	8/15	9/16	10/17		
7/21	8/18	9/21	10/26		
7/23	8/21	9/25			
	8/24	9/28			
	8/28				

Jan. 1998	Feb. 1998	March 1998	April 1998	May 1998	June 1998
1/8	2/1	3/4	4/16	5/1	6/1
1/26	2/7	3/10	4/23	5/8	6/7
	2/16	3/19		5/14	6/14
	2/25	3/29		5/22	6/21
					6/28

July 1998	Aug. 1998	Sept. 1998	Oct. 1998	Nov. 1998	Dec. 1998
7/4	8/2	9/5	10/4	11/10	12/7
7/12	8/9	9/13	10/13	11/16	12/14
7/22	8/16	9/20	10/19	11/24	12/21
7/28	8/24	9/27	10/26	11/30	12/27
	8/31		10/31		

Jan. 1999	Feb. 1999	March 1999	April 1999	May 1999	June 1999
1/6	2/9	3/1	4/5	5/3	6/8
1/11	2/12	3/7	4/11	5/16	
1/18	2/22	3/21	4/20	5/23	
1/20		3/29	4/26	5/31	
1/31					

July 1999	Aug. 1999	Sept. 1999	Oct. 1999	Nov. 1999	Dec. 1999
7/3	8/8	9/2	10/11	11/3	12/1
7/30		9/22	10/28	11/19	12/15
				11/28	12/20

*Jan. 2000	Feb. 2000	March 2000
1/1	2/8	3/8
1/3 103° temperature		
1/4 Fever completely gone within 8 hrs.		
1/21		

*This is the year that I drastically cut back on colonics but should not have. Less colonics caused the heavy metals to back up into the kidneys.

*April 2000	May 2000	June 2000	July 2000	Aug. 2000	Sept. 2000	Oct. 2000	Nov. 2000	Dec. 2000
4/2	5/8	6/24	7/5	8/1	9/7	10/6	11/18	12/2
4/17	5/27		7/16	8/2	9/12	10/17		12/13
4/29				8/18	9/14	10/31		12/23
					9/21			

Jan. 2001	Feb. 2001	March 2001	**April 2001	May 2001	June 2001
1/5	2/19	3/8	4/1	5/2	6/1
1/25		3/15	4/2	5/7	6/3
1/27		3/20	4/3	5/12	6/7
		3/22	4/5	5/16	6/11
		3/27	4/7	5/21	6/15
		3/28	4/9	5/23	6/19
		3/29	4/11		6/22
		3/30	4/13		6/24
		3/31	4/15		
			4/17		
			4/18		
			4/22		
			4/23		
			4/24		
			4/26		
			4/28		

**July 2001	Aug. 2001	Sept. 2001	Oct. 2001	Nov. 2001	Dec. 2001
7/4	8/3	9/7	10/5	11/6	12/7
7/9	8/10	9/15	10/12	11/13	12/14
7/12	8/15	9/22	10/18	11/17	12/16
7/18	8/24	9/29	10/24	11/23	12/21
	8/31		10/30	11/29	

  **These months, starting in 4/01, is when I stepped up the colonics because of the septic state. The heavy metals were released from all areas of my body into my kidneys. The kidneys were able to release the heavy metals into the bowel and out of the body, because of the colonics. Now I was out of danger.

Jan. 2002	Feb. 2002	March 2002	April 2002	May 2002	June 2002
1/13	2/6	3/1	4/15	5/1	6/1
1/18	2/12		4/22	5/7	6/4
1/29	2/19			5/14	6/5
	2/25			5/21	6/7
				5/29	6/8
				5/30	6/9
				5/31	6/10
					6/11
					6/12
					6/13
					6/15
					6/17
					6/18
					6/19
					6/20
					6/21
					6/22
					6/23
					6/24
					6/25
					6/26
					6/28
					6/30

July 2002	Aug. 2002	Sept. 2002	Oct. 2002	Nov. 2002	Dec. 2002
7/1	8/1	9/2	10/6	11/5	12/1
7/2	8/2	9/4	10/11	11/9	12/6
7/4	8/3	9/8	10/14	11/15	12/11
7/6	8/5	9/11	10/24	11/21	12/16
7/8	8/7	9/14	10/31	11/26	12/21
7/10	8/9	9/17			12/26
7/12	8/12	9/19			
7/17	8/14	9/21			
7/16	8/16	9/23			
7/18	8/18	9/26			
7/20	8/20	9/31			
7/22	8/23				
7/24					
7/26					
7/28					
7/30					

Jan. 2003	Feb. 2003	March 2003	April 2003
1/23	2/6	3/6	4/6
1/28	2/12	3/13	4/10
	2/17	3/18	4/21
	2/22	3/29	4/26
	2/27		